# A ROOKIE READER

# KATIE DID IT

### By Becky Bring McDaniel

### Illustrations by Lois Axeman

Prepared under the direction of Robert Hillerich, Ph.D.

 CHILDRENS PRESS ™

CHICAGO

*Dedicated with all my love
to my husband, Larry and
our three children.*

**Library of Congress Cataloging in Publication Data**

McDaniel, Becky Bring.
  Katie did it.

  (A Rookie reader)
  Includes index.
  Summary: Katie, the youngest of three children, who gets the blame for
everything bad, does something good for a change.
  [1. Brothers and sisters—Fiction.  2. Behavior—Fiction]  I. Axeman, Lois,
ill.  II. Title.  III. Series.  PZ7.M478417Kat 1983    [E]      83-7260
ISBN 0-516-02043-9

Katie was little.

4

Her brother Kris was bigger.

And her sister Jenny
was even bigger.

Whenever milk was spilled,

9

Kris and Jenny said…"Katie did it!"

Whenever the ball was left out,

13

Kris and Jenny said ... "Katie did it!"

When the light was left on,

Jenny and Kris said..."Katie did it!"

When the door was left open,

21

22

Jenny and Kris said..."Katie did it!"

"Katie did it, Katie did it,"
that was all Katie heard.

That day mommy called
Jenny, Kris, and Katie inside.

She asked, "Who gave
me the pretty flowers?"

And do you know
what Katie did?

Katie said, "Katie did it!"

# WORD LIST

| | | |
|---|---|---|
| all | her | |
| and | inside | out |
| asked | it | pretty |
| ball | Jenny | said |
| bigger | Katie | she |
| brother | know | sister |
| called | Kris | spilled |
| day | left | the |
| did | light | that |
| do | little | was |
| door | me | what |
| even | milk | when |
| flowers | mommy | whenever |
| gave | on | who |
| heard | open | you |

## About the Author

Becky Bring McDaniel was born in Ashland, Ohio but spent approximately half her life in Gainesville, Florida where she is pursuing a degree in creative writing at the University of Florida. Several of her poems have been published in such magazines as *Creative Years*, *The National Girl Scout Magazine*, and *Writers' Opportunities*. She is married and has three children ranging in ages from five to nine years old. She has several other manuscripts in progress and looks forward to a career in writing for children.

## About the Artist

Lois Axeman was born and raised in Chicago, Illinois. She studied art in Chicago at the American Academy, Illinois Institute of Technology, and at the Art Institute. She taught illustration at the University of Illinois Circle Campus for four years. The mother of two grown children and grandmother of one, Lois and her husband, Harvey Retzloff, live on the fifty-fourth floor of a lakefront building where they both pursue their careers in the graphic arts. They share their home with their Shih Tzu dog Marty and their female cat Charlie. Lois uses her children, her grandchild, and her pets as models for her picture book characters. In their spare time Lois and Harvey enjoy painting, playing tennis, and growing orchids.